SECRETS OF DARK WEB

The Darkest Side Of The Dark Web:

All You Need To Know About the Darknet

By

Dr Ken Graham

Table Of Content

Chapter 5: Things You Need to Know About the Dark Web

Chapter 6: Advantages and Disadvantages of the Dark Web

- **How Does Dark Web Help Cyber Security Experts Improve Business Security**

- **Ways Cyber Security Experts Use the Dark Web to Help Protect Businesses From Hacker Threats.**

Conclusion

Introduction

The term "dark web" describes
purposefully concealed content on the
internet that can only be accessed
with specialised software like Tor
Browser. The deep web, which is all
online content that isn't indexed by
search engines, includes the dark web
as a subset.

The darknet, a portion of the internet
that is both not indexed by search
engines and only accessible using a
browser like Tor or through particular
network setups, is where the dark

web's content is located. The "dark" portion here refers to the employment of particular software to access the dark web, which maintains your anonymity.

The dark internet uses numerous web servers to distribute online information and encrypts communications to maintain user anonymity. even though the dark web

Chapter 1

Dark Web

The dark web is a part of the internet that isn't indexed by search engines and requires the use of an anonymizing browser called For to be accessed. You've no doubt heard talk of the "dark web" as a hotbed of criminal activity — and it is. Researchers Daniel Moore and Thomas Rid of King's College in London classified the contents of 2,723 live dark web sites over a five-week period in 2015 and found that 57% host illicit material.

A 2019 study, Into the Web of Profit, conducted by Dr. Michael McGuires at the University of Surrey, shows that things have become worse. The number of dark web listings that could harm an enterprise has risen by 20% since 2016. Of all listings (excluding those selling drugs), 60% could potentially harm enterprises.

You can buy credit card numbers, all manner of drugs, guns, counterfeit money, stolen subscription credentials, hacked Netflix accounts and software that helps you break into other people's computers. Buy login credentials to a $50,000 Bank of America account, counterfeit $20 bills, prepaid debit cards, or a "lifetime" Netflix premium account. You can hire hackers to attack computers for you. You can buy usernames and passwords.

Not everything is illegal, the dark web also has a legitimate side. For example, you can join a chess club or BlackBook, a social network described as "the Facebook of Tor."

Difference Between Deep Web And Dark Web:

Although they are sometimes used interchangeably, the terms "deep web" and "dark web" are not the same thing.

Anything on the internet that is not indexed by a search engine like Google is referred to as the Deep Web. Anything that is behind a paywall or requires login credentials is deep web content. Additionally, it includes content whose owners have prevented web crawlers from indexing it.

The Deep Web

The deep web includes, among other things, confidential corporate websites, membership websites, fee-based content, medical records, and so on. The deep web accounts for between 96% and 99% of the internet, according to estimates. A standard web browser can only access a small portion of the internet—commonly referred to as the "clear web."

The majority of digital content on the internet cannot be found using web search engines.

This enormous amount of data can be found on the Deep Web, also known as the "hidden web," where nearly all online activities take place.

The Deep Web is actually a part of your daily routine. You are always on the Deep Web when you use social media, check your online banking information, or log into your email account.

For security and privacy reasons, access to information on the Deep Web typically requires a username and password.

The Deep Web's entities include:

Databases, apps for social media, banking online, email, intranets, forums, content behind a paywall

The Dark Web

The Dark Web is a subset of the deep web that is intentionally hidden and can only be accessed through a particular browser, Tor, as will be discussed below. The dark web's actual size is unknown, but the majority of estimates put it at around 5% of the internet's total. Again, despite its ominous name, not all of the dark web is used for illegal activities.

There are millions of websites, databases, and servers that are all active around-the-clock on the vast Internet. Yet, the sites that can be accessed using search engines like Google and Yahoo are only the tip of the iceberg when it comes to the so-called "visible" Internet (also known as the surface web or open web).

The non-visible Web is surrounded by a number of terminologies, but if you're going to venture off the beaten track, it's important to understand how they differ.

Open Web Or Surface Web

The "visible" surface layer is the open web, often known as the surface web. The open web would be the top part that is above the sea if we were to continue to picture the full web as an iceberg. In terms of statistics, this collection of websites and data falls under 5% of all internet traffic.

This page contains all of the websites that are frequently viewed by the general public and can be accessed using standard browsers like Internet Explorer, Google Chrome, and Firefox. Websites are typically identified by registry operators like ".com" and ".org," making them simple to locate using common search engines.

Search engines can index the web through visible links—a process known as "crawling" because the search engine travels the web like a spider—making it possible to locate surface web websites.

The deep web: About 90% of all websites can be found in the deep web, which lies below the surface. This would be the much larger submerged portion of an iceberg than the web on the surface. In fact, it is impossible to precisely determine the number of active pages or websites at any given time because this hidden web is so vast.

The analogy could be extended to say that large search engines are like fishing boats that can only "catch" websites close to the surface. Academic journals, private databases, and additional illicit content are all out of reach. The dark web, which is a subset of this deep web, is also a part of it.

Even though a lot of media outlets use the terms "deep web" and "dark web" interchangeably, a lot of the deep part is perfectly legal and safe. The deep web's largest components include:

Databases: both publicly accessible and privately protected file collections that can only be searched within the database itself and are not connected to any other areas of the internet.

Intranets: used to privately communicate and control aspects within their organisations by businesses, governments, and educational institutions.

If you're wondering how to get to the deep web, you probably use it every day. All web pages that search engines cannot identify are referred to as the "deep web." Some deep websites tell search engines not to "crawl" them, while others are hidden behind passwords or other security barriers. These pages are more hidden due to the absence of visible links.

The content that is "hidden" on the larger deep web is typically safer and cleaner. The deep web includes everything from the pages you access when you bank online to blog posts that are currently under review and awaiting redesign. In addition, neither your computer nor general safety are in jeopardy from these. The majority of these pages are hidden from the public internet in order to safeguard user privacy and information, such as:

Email and social messaging accounts Private enterprise databases HIPAA-sensitive information like medical records Legal files Exploring further into the deep web does bring a little bit more risk to the surface. Parts of the deep web make it possible for some users to circumvent local restrictions and access services like television and movies that may not be available in their area. Others go a little further, downloading pirated music or stealing unreleased movies.

The most risky content and activities can be found on the dark side of the internet. The Tor websites can only be accessed through an anonymous browser at this extreme end of the deep web, which is also known as the "dark web."

Because you might accidentally end up in dangerous areas, deep web safety is more important to the average internet user than dark web safety: Normal internet browsers can still access many parts of the deep web. Users can end up on a pirated website, a politically radical forum, or a disturbingly violent content if they travel through enough tangential pathways.

The term "dark web" refers to websites that cannot be found in search engines and can only be accessed through specialised web browsers. The dark web is considered a component of the deep web because it is significantly smaller than the tiny surface web. The dark web would be represented as the tip of the iceberg that is submerged using our ocean and iceberg illustration.

However, the dark web is a very hidden part of the deep web that very few people will ever interact with or even see. To put it another way, the dark web is included in the deep web, which encompasses everything below the surface that can still be accessed using the appropriate software.

The dark web's structure can be deconstructed to reveal a few key components that make it an anonymous haven:

There is no surface web search engine indexing of web pages. Pages on the dark web cannot be found or displayed by Google and other popular search engines.

Through a randomly generated network infrastructure, "virtual traffic tunnels."

due to its unique registry operator, it is inaccessible to standard browsers. It is further obscured by encryption and firewalls, two network security measures.

The dark web's reputation has often been linked to sites where users can buy illegal goods or services or to criminal intent or content. However, this framework has also been utilised by legal parties.

Dark web dangers are very different from deep web dangers in terms of safety. It's not always easy to find illegal cyber activity, but if you do, it tends to be much more extreme and dangerous. Let's look at how and why people access these websites before discussing the dangers posed by the dark web.

Chapter 2

How To Access The Dark Web

In the past, cybercriminals, law enforcement, and hackers controlled the dark web. However, anyone who is interested can now dive into the dark using new technology like encryption and the anonymization browser software Tor.

Users can access websites using the Tor network browser, also known as

"The Onion Routing." onion operator in the registry. The United States Naval Research Laboratory created this browser as a service in the latter part of the 1990s.

An early version of Tor was created to conceal spy communications because it was realised that the nature of the internet meant there was no privacy. The framework was eventually repurposed, and the browser we know today has since been made available to the public. It is available for free download to everyone.

Think of Tor as a web browser like Firefox or Google Chrome. Notably, the Tor browser uses a random path of encrypted servers known as "nodes" rather than the most direct route between your computer and the deep parts of the web. Users are now able to connect to the deep web without worrying about their browser history or actions being tracked.

Sites on the deep web also use Tor (or software that is similar to it, like I2P, the "Invisible Internet Project") to keep their identities a secret. This means that you won't be able to figure out who runs them or where they are hosted.

What exactly is Tor?

Tor is a web browser for accessing the dark web and remaining anonymous online. Tor is similar to VPNs and proxy servers in that they all provide some level of anonymity for web browsing. When combined with a virtual private network (VPN), Tor can provide powerful, overlapping levels of privacy and anonymity.

The Tor Project is the most popular way to access content on the Dark Web. It was created in the middle of the 1990s to shield communications between U.S. intelligence agencies from prying eyes.

To guarantee complete anonymity, the Onion Router—hence the name Tor—utilises a unique internet traffic routing mechanism and three layers of encryption. It has the ability to bounce internet traffic around the Tor relay network at random and has strong encryption layers.

The purpose of this high entry barrier to the Dark Web is to safeguard user identities, online activities, and locations while preserving their anonymity.

Internet users can use the Dark Web to communicate and share confidential data without being tracked by using the Tor browser. To further conceal themselves, the majority of Dark Web users are logged into a Virtual Private Network (VPN).

The Tor Project and Freenet are incorrectly referred to as synonyms for the Dark Web. In order to safeguard online communications, the Tor network and other networks employing onion routing emerged. not to back illegal activities.

Is it against the law to use the dark web?

To put it simply, it is not against the law to access the dark web. In fact, there are some uses that are perfectly legal and support the "dark web's" value. On the dull web, clients can search out three clear advantages from its utilisation:

The dark web has attracted a large number of parties who would otherwise be put in danger by disclosing their identities online due to its user anonymity and virtually untraceable services and websites. Whistleblowers, victims of abuse and persecution, and political dissidents have all made frequent use of these hidden websites. However, these advantages can easily be extended to those who wish to act in other explicitly illegal ways outside of the confines of laws.

When viewed through this prism, the way you interact with the dark web determines its legality. There are a lot of important reasons why you might get sidetracked by legal lines and lose your freedom. In order to ensure the safety and protection of others, others may engage in illegal behaviour. Let's discuss both of these ideas in terms of websites and the "dark web browser."

Is Tor against the law?

The use of Tor and other anonymized browsers is not strictly prohibited on the software end. In point of fact, these so-called "dark web" browsers are not only bound to this section of the internet. Tor is now used by many users to browse both the public Internet and more private areas of the web.

In the digital age of today, the Tor browser's privacy features are crucial. Unauthorised online activity surveillance is currently carried out by corporations and governing bodies alike. While others have no choice, some simply do not want government agencies or even Internet Service Providers (ISPs) to know what they are looking at online. Even public websites can't be accessed by users in countries with strict access and user laws unless they use Tor clients and virtual private networks (VPNs).

Despite the browser's legality, you can still engage in illegal activities within Tor that could bring you into legal trouble. You could easily use Tor to pirate content from the deep web that is protected by law, share illegal pornography, or carry out cyberterrorism. Your actions will not fall under the law if you use a legal browser.

Is it against the law to use and visit dark web sites?

The dark web is more of a grey area on the network side. Most of the time, using the dark web means that you want to do something you wouldn't normally be able to do in public.

If their true identities were discovered, critics of the government and other outspoken advocates may be concerned about negative reactions. People who have been harmed by others might not want their attackers to hear about their conversations about the incident. It would be illegal if the governing bodies you belong to deemed an activity to be illegal.

However, criminals and malicious hackers also prefer to operate in the shadows, so anonymity has its drawbacks. Cyberattacks and human trafficking, for instance, are activities that participants are aware will be damaging. Because of this, they take these actions to the dark web to hide.

In the end, it is not unlawful to merely browse these areas, but doing so may cause problems for you. Unsavoury activity does exist in many areas of the dark web, despite the fact that it is not entirely forbidden. If you are not vigilant or an experienced, computer-savvy user aware of its vulnerabilities, it can expose you to unneeded risks. So what does the dark web do when it's being used for crime?

Tools and services from the Web of Profit report, 12 different kinds of tools and services were identified as potentially posing a threat in the form of a breach of the network or the compromise of data:

Access, such as keyloggers, exploits, and remote access Trojans (RATs); malware, distributed denial of service (DDoS), and botnet infections or attacks services, customization, and targeting as examples of espionage; services such as tutorials and support Credentials; Phishing; Refunds; Data on customers; data from operations;

monetary data; property intellectual; as well as Other New Threats. Additionally, the report outlined three risk factors for each category:

Ransomware-as-a-service (RaaS) kits have been available on the dark web for several years, but those offerings have become much more dangerous with the rise of specialised criminal groups like REvil or GandCrab. Devaluing the enterprise could mean undermining brand trust, causing damage to the reputation, or losing ground to a competitor. Disrupting the enterprise could mean DDoS attacks or other malware that affects business operations. Frauding the enterprise could mean IP theft or e These groups create their own sophisticated malware and distribute it through "affiliates," sometimes combining it with tools that already exist.

The ransomware packages are distributed by affiliates via the dark web. The theft of victims' data and the threat to release it on the dark web if the ransom is not paid are common features of these attacks.

This business strategy is effective and profitable. For instance, IBM Security X-Force reported that REvil was involved in 29% of its 2020 ransomware engagements. Affiliates pay the criminal organisations that developed the malware a cut of the profits, which typically ranges from 20% to 30%. REvil's profits last year, according to IBM, were $81 million.

With all of this activity and the image of a bustling market, you might think it's easy to navigate the dark web. It's not. When everyone is anonymous and a significant portion of them are attempting to defraud others, the place is as messy and chaotic as you would expect.

To get to the dark web, you need to use Tor, a browser that keeps you anonymous. Your web page requests are routed through a network of proxy servers managed by thousands of volunteers worldwide by the Tor browser, rendering your IP address unrecognisable and untraceable. Tor works like magic, but the end result is the same as the dark web: erratic, unreliable, and incredibly slow

However, the dark web offers a memorable glimpse into the murky underbelly of human existence—without the risk of skulking around in a dark alley—to those who are willing to put up with the inconvenience.

Dark web search engine Although there are dark web search engines, even the best of them struggle to keep up with the ever-changing landscape. The experience is comparable to browsing the internet in the latter part of the 1990s. Even Grams, one of the best search engines, returns results that are often irrelevant to the query and repetitive. Another option is to use link lists like The Hidden Wiki, but even indexes give you a lot of timed-out connections and 404 errors, which is annoying.

Websites on the dark web resemble other websites in appearance, but there are significant distinctions. The naming structure is one. Dark web websites don't end in.com or.co; instead, they end in.onion. According to Wikipedia, that is "a special-use top level domain suffix designating an anonymous hidden service reachable via the Tor network." These websites can be accessed by browsers that use the appropriate proxy, but not by others.

Additionally, dark web websites employ a jumbled naming convention, resulting in URLs that are frequently difficult to recall. For instance, the popular e-commerce site Dream Market has an address that is hard to understand: "eajwlvm3z2lcca76.onion."

Scammers have set up a lot of dark websites, and they always change places to avoid getting in trouble with their victims. If the owners decide to cash in and flee with the escrow funds they are holding on behalf of customers, even commerce websites that have existed for more than a year can vanish suddenly.

The ability of law enforcement to locate and prosecute owners of websites that sell illegal goods and services is improving. AlphaBay, the largest illicit marketplace on the dark web, was successfully shut down in the summer of 2017 by a team of cyber cops from three nations, shaking the network. However, many merchants simply relocated.

According to Keeper Security's Director of Security & Architecture and resident expert on the subject, Patrick Tiquet, "The Tor network's anonymity also makes it especially vulnerable to DDoS." It's a very dynamic environment because sites constantly change addresses to avoid DDoS, he said. "The quality of search varies greatly, and a lot of material is outdated," as a result.

The dark web has flourished thanks to bitcoin, the crypto-currency that enables two parties to conduct a trusted transaction without knowing each other's identity. "Bitcoin has been a major factor in the growth of the dark web, and the dark web has been a big factor in the growth of bitcoin," says Tiquet.

Nearly all dark web commerce sites conduct transactions in bitcoin or some variant, but that doesn't mean it's safe to do business there. The inherent anonymity of the place attracts scammers and thieves, but what do you expect when buying guns or drugs is your objective?

Dark web commerce sites have the same features as any e-retail operation, including ratings/reviews, shopping carts and forums, but there are important differences. One is quality control. When both buyers and sellers are anonymous, the credibility of any ratings system is dubious. Ratings are easily manipulated, and even sellers with long track records have been known to suddenly disappear with their customers' crypto-coins, only to set up shop later under a different alias.

Most e-commerce providers offer some kind of escrow service that keeps customer funds on hold until the product has been delivered. However, in the event of a dispute don't expect service with a smile. It's pretty much up to the buyer and the seller to duke it out. Every communication is encrypted, so even the simplest transaction requires a PGP key.

Even completing a transaction is no guarantee that the goods will arrive.

Many need to cross international borders, and customs officials are cracking down on suspicious packages. The dark web news site Deep.Dot.Web teems with stories of buyers who have been arrested or jailed for attempted purchases.

As in the real world, the price you pay for stolen data fluctuates as the market changes. According to Privacy Affair's Dark Web Price Index 2021, these are the most current prices for some of the data and services commonly traded over the dark web:

Cloned credit card with PIN: $25 to
$35

Credit card details with account
balance up to $5,000: $240

Stolen online banking logins with at
least $2,000 in the account: $120

PayPal transfers from stolen accounts:
$50 to $340
Hacked Coinbase verified account:
$610

Hacked social media account: $1 to
$60

Hacked Gmail account: $80

Hacked eBay account with good reputation: $1,000

Is The Dark Web Illegal?
We don't want to leave you with the impression that everything on the dark web is nefarious or illegal. The Tor network began as an anonymous communications channel, and it still serves a valuable purpose in helping people communicate in environments that are hostile to free speech. "A lot of

people use it in countries where there's eavesdropping or where internet access is criminalised," Tiquet said.

If you want to learn all about privacy protection or cryptocurrency, the dark web has plenty to offer. There are a variety of private and encrypted email services, instructions for installing an anonymous operating system and advanced tips for the privacy-conscious.

There's also material that you wouldn't be surprised to find on the public web, such as links to full-text editions of hard-to-find books, collections of political news from mainstream websites and a guide to the steam tunnels under the Virginia Tech campus. You can conduct discussions about current events anonymously on Intel Exchange. There are several whistleblower sites, including a dark web version of Wikileaks. Pirate Bay, a BitTorrent site that law enforcement officials have repeatedly shut down, is alive and well there. Even Facebook has a dark web presence.

"More and more legitimate web companies are starting to have presences there," Tiquet said. "It shows that they're aware, they're cutting edge and in the know."

There's also plenty of practical value for some organisations. Law enforcement agencies keep an ear to the ground on the dark web looking for stolen data from recent security breaches that might lead to a trail to the perpetrators. Many mainstream media organisations monitor whistleblower sites looking for news.

Staying on top of the hacker underground

Keeper's Patrick Tiquet checks in regularly because it's important for him to be on top of what's happening in the hacker underground. "I use the dark web for situational awareness, threat analysis and keeping an eye on what's going on," he said. "I want to know what information is available and have an external lens into the digital assets that are being monetized – this gives us insight on what hackers are targeting."

If you find your own information on the dark web, there's precious little you can do about it, but at least you'll know you've been compromised. Bottom line: If you can tolerate the lousy performance, unpredictable availability, and occasional shock factor of the dark web, it's worth a visit. Just don't buy anything there.

Chapter 3

Types Of Threats On The Dark Web

On the off chance that you're thinking about involving the dark web for fundamental security purposes you could in any case address, "Is dark web risky to utilise?" Sadly, it particularly can be a hazardous spot to be. The following are a few normal dangers you might look during your perusing encounters:

1. Pernicious programming

Pernicious programming — for example malware — is completely alive all over the dull web. It is in many cases presented in certain entries to give danger entertainers the apparatuses for cyberattacks. Be that as it may, it additionally waits the whole way across the dark web to taint clueless clients very much as it does on the remainder of the web.

The dull web doesn't convey as a significant number of the common agreements that site suppliers follow to safeguard clients on the remainder of the web. In that capacity, clients can end up consistently presented to certain sorts of malware like:

Keyloggers

Botnet malware

Ransomware

Phishing malware

Assuming you decide to seek after investigating any locales on the dim web, you put yourself in danger of being singled out and focused on for hacks and that's just the beginning. Most malware diseases can be gotten by your endpoint security programs.

The dangers of internet perusing can reach out into the turned off world on the off chance that your PC or arrange association can be taken advantage of. Secrecy is strong with Pinnacle and the structure of the dull web, however it isn't dependable. Any internet based action can convey breadcrumbs to your personality assuming somebody digs adequately far.

2. Government observing

With numerous Pinnacle based locales being surpassed by police specialists across the globe, there is an unmistakable risk of becoming government focus for essentially visiting a dim site.

Unlawful medication commercial centres like the Silk Street have been captured for police reconnaissance previously. By using custom programming to invade and investigate action, this has permitted regulation authorities to find client characters of supporters and spectators the same. Regardless of whether you never make a buy, you could be watched and implicate yourself for different exercises sometime down the road.

Invasions can endanger you by observing different kinds of action too. Avoiding government limitations to investigate new political philosophies can be an imprisonable offence in certain nations. China utilises what is known as the "Incomparable Firewall" to limit admittance to famous locales for this definite explanation. The gamble of being a guest to this content could prompt being put on a watchlist or quick focusing for a prison sentence.

3. Scam

A few claimed administrations like the expert "contract killers" may simply be trick (scam)

Some alleged services, like professional "hitmen," might just be rip-offs meant to make money off of willing customers. The dark web is said to provide a variety of illegal services, including paid assassinations, sex trafficking, and weapons trafficking.

In this section of the internet, some of these are well-known threats that have been around for some time. However, it's possible that others are taking advantage of the dark web's reputation to defraud users of substantial sums of money. Also, some people on the dark web might try phishing scams to get your personal information or identity for money.

Protection for end users from being exploited by the dark web Regardless of whether you use the internet for business, as a parent, or for any other purpose, you should take precautions to keep your private life and information off the dark web.

If you want to prevent the misuse of your private information, monitoring for identity theft is essential. Any kind of personal information can be sold online for a profit. On the dark web, passwords, physical addresses, bank account numbers, and social security numbers are frequently traded. You may already be aware that these can be used by criminals to harm your credit, steal money, and breach other online accounts. Social fraud can also harm your reputation when personal data is leaked.

In order to stop malicious actors from exploiting you, antivirus and antimalware protections are equally important. Malware-infected users steal a lot of information from the dark web. Your data can be gathered by attackers using keyloggers, and they can get into your system anywhere on the internet. Endpoint security applications like Kaspersky Security

Cloud cover identity monitoring and anti-virus protection all in one place.

How to stay safe when using the dark web If you have a valid reason to use the dark web, you should take precautions to ensure your safety.

7 Safe Ways to Access the Dark Web

1. Trust Your Senses. You need to be careful online if you want to avoid being taken advantage of. Everyone is not as they appear. Watching who you talk to and where you go is essential for safety. If something doesn't feel right, you should always act to get out of a situation.

2. Separate your online identity from your real one.
You should never use your username, email address, "real name," password, or even credit

card anywhere else in your life. If necessary, create brand-new disposable accounts and identifiers for yourself. Before making any purchases, acquire prepaid debit cards that cannot be identified. Use nothing online or in person that could be used to identify you.

3. Use active surveillance for identity and money theft. For your safety, numerous online security services now offer identity protection. If you have

access to these tools, you should make sure to use them.

4. Do not download files from the dark web in any way. The lawless realm of the dark web is marked by a significantly higher level of concern regarding malware infection. If you decide to download anything, an antivirus program's real-time file scanning can help you check any new files.

5. In any network settings that are available, disable Java and ActiveX. It is common practice for malicious parties to investigate and take advantage of these frameworks. You should avoid this risk because you are travelling through a network that is full of those threats.

6. For all of your daily activities, use a secondary non-admin local user account. On most computers, the native account will have full administrative

rights by default. The majority of malware must utilise this to carry out its functions. Accordingly, you can slow or stop the advancement of abuse by restricting the record being used to severe honours.

7. Limit who can access your Tor-enabled device at all times. Make sure your children or other members of the family are safe so they won't accidentally stumble upon something no one should ever see. If you're interested, go to

the Deep Web, but keep kids
away from it.

Services And Tools For The Dark Web

Although browsing the dark web is not as simple as browsing the regular web, you can use a few tools to plot your course. You can find trustworthy dark websites by using dark web search engines and forums like Reddit, but you will need a dark web browser to visit them.

Dark web browsers Tor Browser is the most common dark web browser. It routes your web traffic through the Tor network to reach the darknet. Your traffic is encrypted and bounced between at least three relay points, or nodes, as it moves through Tor. This helps hide where the data came from and makes it difficult for anyone to find your IP address. However, as a result, Tor Browser will appear to be significantly slower than a standard web browser.

Dark web search engines Although surface web search engines are unable to access the dark web, specialised dark web search engines can assist you in locating the information you require. DuckDuckGo is a well-known search engine that prioritises privacy and does not track you when you use it. The pages on the dark web are indexed by DuckDuckGo's dark web search engine; however, Tor Browser is required to view them.

Not Evil, Torch, Haystack, and Ahmia are additional dark web search engines. If you want to learn how to search the dark and deep webs for the content you want, the subreddit r/deepweb is a good place to start. Last but not least, The Hidden Wiki is a collection of links from the dark web. However, the links might not work and lead to risky websites.

Dark websites require a specific dark web browser to access, and the majority of dark web URLs are strings of letters and numbers that appear to be randomly generated, in contrast to the surface web's simple web addresses.

A surface website called the Hidden Wiki provides a collection of links to the dark web; however, the links don't always work and may not be safe. Make use of it to get an idea of the kinds of dark websites you might find interesting. However, in order to safeguard yourself from any threats

you may encounter, purchase
comprehensive cybersecurity software
prior to visiting any dark web sites.

Chapter 4

Why Is There The Dark Web?

It is now referred to as the shady source of numerous security issues in mainstream discussions about technology and digital security.

The Dark Web essentially makes use of a group of nodes and networks known as "darknets." Peer-to-peer networks of all sizes, including Tor and Freenet, fall under this category.

Users of specialised software, such as the Tor browser, are required if they wish to browse and utilise the Dark Web. It's important to know how and why this Dark Web browser works because it plays such a significant role in online activity.

The following individuals require the Dark Web in order to continue performing their hazardous, but not necessarily illegal, work:

Dissidents of oppressive regimes, activists, journalists, and law enforcement intelligence agencies are all examples of whistleblowers. As you might expect, misinformed individuals or those who clearly intend to commit a crime have found a way to use this level of anonymity to conceal their illicit activities and, up to a point, evade law enforcement agencies.

Why Does the Dark Web Present Such Risks? What Are My Options There?

In a variety of illegal ways, cybercriminals and other malicious actors heavily rely on the Dark Web's capabilities. Marketplaces and forums where criminals transact illegally are the Dark Web's hotspots for illegal activity.

On these black markets, criminals and con artists sell a variety of illegal goods, including stolen and counterfeit data:

Personal data. This includes full names, home addresses, phone numbers, birth dates, Social Security numbers, hacked email addresses, and many other details that can be used to identify you. It is also known as PII, or personally identifiable information.

Financial data. stolen information about credit cards, usernames and passwords for online banking, credentials for cryptocurrency accounts, banking and insurance records, and many other things.

Login data for an online account. typically consisting of a username and password combination that grants access to paid professional services, ride-sharing and video streaming services, and social media accounts. Even antivirus and genetic testing product logins are in high demand.

Medical records. This includes your medical history, prescriptions, biometric data (such as fingerprints and images of your face), test results, billing information, and other sensitive details (also known as PHI or personal health information). This can lead to fingerprint identity theft or even medical identity theft in the wrong hands.

confidential company information. includes operational details, competitive intelligence, intellectual property, and other classified information.

Fashioned information. Particularly bank drafts, stolen IDs and driver's licences, and counterfeit passports.

Other illicit marketplaces on the Dark Web These black markets not only offer illegal drugs, access to emerging cyber threats and viruses, and even hitmen for hire, but they also offer personal information obtained from data breaches, various other kinds of cyber attacks, and online scams.

Silk Road, the most well-known Dark Web marketplace, served over 100,000 customers at its peak.

The website, which Ross Ulbricht started in 2011, became the most popular black market, especially among drug traffickers. In 2013, the FBI took down Silk Road, but version 2.0 briefly returned before being taken down permanently.

Along with three other convictions, Ross Ulbricht received two life terms. Throughout the entire takedown operation and the decade that followed, the United States government seized bitcoin worth more than $1 billion.

People look for the Dark Web for a variety of reasons, not the least of which is the chance to make a lot of money on these Dark Web marketplaces. Additionally, a significant amount of child pornography can be found on this section of the internet, with some websites attracting tens or hundreds of thousands of visitors.

The Dark Web offers more than just "products" to anyone willing to buy and consume because it serves as a hub for criminal activity. Additionally, it provides services that make it possible for cybercriminals to launch attacks without requiring extensive technical expertise.

Historical Backdrop Of The Dark Web

The arrival of Freenet in 2000 is in many cases referred to as the start of the dull web. The Freenet was Ian Clarke's thesis project at the University of Edinburgh in Scotland. It was designed as a way to communicate, share files, and interact online anonymously.

The release of the Tor network in 2002, supported by researchers from the US Naval Research Laboratory, significantly expanded the dark web.

Since the internet was still in its infancy at the time, it was simple to identify individuals while remaining anonymous. The purpose of the Tor network was to provide secure means of communication for political dissidents and American intelligence agents worldwide.

A nonprofit organisation known as the Tor Project was established after the underlying code of Tor was made available for free. The Tor Browser was released in 2008, making it simple for anyone to access the dark web.

How large is the dark web?

Despite its apparent size, the dark web is actually quite small. Recorded Future researchers estimated that only 8,400 of the over 55,000 onion domains that were already in existence—roughly 15%—were currently active. This indicates that the total size of the live dark web network is only 0.005 percent of the surface web.

Dark web domains typically behave inconsistently—new ones appear and then vanish—which makes sense given that some of these websites may be selling illegal or questionable goods and services.

According to the Tor Project, only 1.5% of the 2 million people who use Tor on a daily basis access hidden or dark websites. Additionally, the vast majority of the dark web's content can be found in English; one estimate states that 78% of the content is available in English.

What is happening today on the dark web?

It's easy to assume that everything that happens on the dark web is illegal due to its emphasis on privacy and anonymity. Even though there is a lot of cybercrime, the dark web is also used legally.

Some people just don't like to share any information online, so they use Tor to access normal websites that aren't on the dark web or dark web news websites and forums.

Is there any illegal use of the dark web?

Yes, many illegal activities are carried out via the dark web. Darknet marketplaces can be used to buy and sell illegal drugs, malware, and illegal content. Weapons and hazardous chemicals are available for purchase on some dark web marketplaces.

Ransomware as a service (RaaS) is a service that cybercriminals use to "rent" ransomware from its creator in exchange for a fee or a percentage of ransom payments. Others sell software exploits that can be used by other cybercriminals to steal personal data and infect victims with malware.

The Silk Road, which launched in 2011 and essentially served as an Amazon-like market for illegal drugs, was the most well-known dark web marketplace. The Silk Road was shut down by the FBI in 2013, and its founder, Ross Ulbricht, is currently serving a double life sentence. The dark web is full of scams and fraud: offers services that are too good to be true and require an upfront payment. Access to email accounts, social media profiles, and other information that can be used to steal an individual's identity is sold by hackers.

With Avast Breachguard, you can safeguard your data from the dark web. Avast BreachGuard will notify you immediately if and when your data is made available for sale by monitoring well-known dark web marketplaces. Before anyone can use your data against you, you can change your passwords and secure your accounts in this way.

Is there danger on the dark web?

As a result of its lack of regulation, the dark web presents a greater risk than the surface web. Scams and malware are dispersed throughout the dark web like landmines. Additionally, it is easier to fall prey to shady websites because of the abundance of unfamiliar-looking dark web sites.

Regular users of the dark web are aware that the site's shady reputation and services can be exploited. Additionally, not all dark web marketplaces provide user reviews, though some do. Scams can easily be carried out by cybercriminals because there is no regulation from authorities or other users.

How safe is the dark web?

It is not always safer to use the dark web than the surface or deep web. Additionally, the increased privacy safeguards of the dark web may actually make it safer, depending on the purpose for which you use it. Follow the recommended security measures, such as using antivirus software and only clicking on links that you can trust, to use the dark web safely. Using a virtual private network (VPN) will enhance security.

On the dark web, can you be tracked ?

On the dark web, it is extremely challenging to monitor online activity. Because you are browsing anonymously, your online activity is hidden when you use Tor, which routes your internet traffic through numerous relay "nodes." Even though Tor supports a variety of privacy extensions, it is still possible to track users on the dark web. Your activities could be tracked if you use personal accounts on the dark web or visit websites with tracking scripts.

Chapter 5

Things You Need to Know About the Dark Web

The world wide web is just the tip of the iceberg when it comes to the content that can be found online. The dark web is buried within the deep web, which extends beyond all of the websites that are indexed by Google and other popular search engines.

Any website that does not appear as a search engine result when users browse content belongs to the second layer of the deep web. A search engine might not index a page for a variety of reasons, including the fact that it is an old page with no obvious keywords or that it is part of an organisation's members-only website. The deep web could also be used to store confidential information, such as documents from the legal or scientific fields, medical records, or information about competitors.

Beyond the deep web is the dark web, a small section of the internet with deliberately hidden websites that can only be accessed through an encrypted browser like Tor or The Onion Router. The following are some facts about the dark web:

1. You must be aware of your search objective.

According to Peraton vice president John M, "the dark web requires a different mindset and skill set." "There are no traditional search engines and algorithms to guide users, so users must have patience to analyse and hunt for the data they are looking for." In addition, the user of the dark web must confirm the relevance of the sources and confirm the accuracy of the information found on specific websites. Outside of public links posted by others, there is no way to stumble upon websites; every action must be deliberate. The dark web is distinct from the surface web because sites, pages, and forums fluctuate, sometimes in a matter of days, adding yet another layer of difficulty in navigation.

2. While searching the dark web, it is simple to infect your machine.

Users of the dark web are less protected because it is not regulated. As a result, clicking links or downloading information makes it simple to infect your computer. John M. cautions, "If you're going to search the dark web, it is best that you do so with a machine you can re-image when you're done." "Many of the websites accessible via a Tor browser are laden with malware." He also mentions that even if a user accesses the information in question by accident, it could still violate federal law to access certain information on the dark web.

3. Smart organisations strengthen security by utilising the dark web.

Services like Peraton's TORNADO can be used by contractors and government agencies to frequently check the dark web to see if anyone is talking about them and what they are saying. Every thirty days, TORNADO automatically and anonymously searches the entire dark web using specific keywords to identify potentially harmful information. Situational awareness can be gained by utilising open source intelligence.

Understanding what kinds of exploits are being performed on one's association permits pioneers to design harm control prior to something occurring. A company can, for instance, conduct a search on the dark web to determine whether any of its internal IP addresses, usernames, or passwords have been made public. In the event of a data breach, it is preferable to be aware of it and take proactive measures before it becomes public.

4. There are Some Advantages To The Dark Web.

The dull web can assist with safeguarding clients' protection in manners the surface web frequently neglects to do. Users can, for instance, share information about what's going on in their country while avoiding government censorship.

Whistleblowers frequently visit the dark web in search of allies who can share their secrets more widely elsewhere.

Doctors were restricted from speaking out about the threat when the COVID-19 outbreak began in Wuhan, China. Information about the outreach was initially censored. Chinese internet users posted updates to the dark web because they were concerned about the virus's potential spread and were aware that it would be much more difficult for their government to locate the leaked information.

5. Rather than being static pages, many dark websites are interactive forums.

There are a lot of locked-down forums on the dark web where people trade and share information. Due to invitation-only access, the average internet user will not be involved in this world. These chat forums typically host the dark web's most sinister activities. As a result, intelligence gathering typically necessitates personal participation in these chat forums in order to obtain the truth. In order to gather evidence for investigations or determine a suspect's identity, federal agencies frequently monitor chat participants who remain anonymous.

Although the dark web makes up only a small portion of the deep web, it presents significant reasons for caution and concern. To safeguard against harm in the future, treasure troves of useful information can be uncovered when safely accessed with TORNADO or another crawler. A valuable asset for any business or government agency is the ability to identify and counteract dark web threats.

Chapter 6

Advantages and Disadvantages of the Dark Web

Advantages

People can freely express their opinions and maintain their privacy thanks to the dark web. For many innocent people who are terrorised by stalkers and other criminals, privacy is essential. It can also be difficult to have open conversations in public due to the increasing tendency of potential employers to monitor social media posts.

One of the benefits of the dark web include the following: Protects privacy and freedom of expression; enables law enforcement to identify criminal organisations;

Last but not least, criminals use the dark web to communicate, which makes it ideal for undercover police officers.

Disadvantage

Some people will unavoidably misuse the power that comes with using the dark web by making it easier to engage in criminal activity. The dark web and cryptocurrencies, for instance, theoretically make it much simpler to hire someone to do certain crimes.

Even though users of the dark web are promised privacy, it can also be used to violate other people's privacy. The dark web has been the target of thefts that have resulted in the dissemination of private data such as medical records, financial information, and private photographs.

It can facilitate criminal activity; and Can be used to violate the privacy of others.

How Does Dark Web Help Cyber Security Experts Improve Business Security

There are good reasons why the term "dark web" has been associated with illegal context. The dark web is the digital marketplace where illegal goods like weapons, drugs, and other items are sold to everyday internet users. The dark web is well-known for hundreds of illegal transactions and activities. This is the dark web's public image.

However, experts in cyber security hold a different perspective. Utilising the dark web has numerous advantages for cyber security professionals. They can learn more about the latest hacking methods by utilising the insights and data that are available on the dark web.

The darknet markets have long been associated with the dark web. However, there is a possibility that not everyone is aware of it. Illicit and illegal activities, as well as billion-dollar business transactions, are frequently referred to as the "darknet market." These things and activities can be found anywhere, and they come in many different forms and go by different names in different countries.

The use of encryption technologies to conceal the information about your business clients' identities, which are used by criminals to buy and sell drugs and other illegal goods, is a distinctive feature of the dark web.

Cyber security experts can open new doors of opportunities and possibilities to improve your organisation's security posture by correctly utilising this technique and others.

The dark web is a section of the internet. It has been linked to criminal activities.

The Federal Bureau of Investigation (FBI) says that dark web surfing is very rare.

The government employees make up the first exception. They can't involve the dull web in the workplace or somewhere else without authorization.

The second exception concerns law enforcement-related work. Within their legal boundaries, law enforcement agencies are permitted to enter any region of the world without revealing their location. This is done so that they can get into these places where the dark web is easy to find.

Law enforcement cyber security specialists can store records and information on the same dark web until a court order is issued. They need a court order before they can access the data of a person. As a result, they are authorised to access the websites' internet domains, where illegal activities have been carried out.

The fact that law enforcement agencies do not require a court order to access any data stored on the dark web is the aspect of this that has generated the most controversy. There is no real way to determine whether these agencies have been abusing their authority in this way.

A child pornographic website was taken down by the FBI a few years ago. They took over the server and installed custom malware that took advantage of a flaw in the Firefox browser, which is the foundation for the Tor browser. This flaw has since been fixed. They then waited.

Customers who had paid for a subscription to the child porn site were infected. The IP address of the computer that downloaded the malware was used by the malware to connect to FBI servers.

Consequently, 900 site users were identified and detained.

Therefore, it is certainly possible to be caught on the dark web. However, it's phenomenally troublesome, and normally requires both the supported exertion of a state-level entertainer and the capacity to find and exploit an imperfection in Peak, a dull web server, or both.

It won't happen unless you do something that would garner such prolonged attention from a state-level actor.

Potential Scope and Benefits of Dark Web for Cybersecurity Experts

There are numerous organisations using the dark web to combat cybercriminals. They have the opportunity to combat cyberspies and hackers via the dark web.

This is primarily because encrypted communication is present. Technology-based communication between two or more people is involved in this. This sets it apart from other methods of communication that do not use encryption technologies to protect privacy and data communication.

Why should businesses be concerned about the dark web?

It is now one of the most talked-about issues in cyber security. This is due to the fact that it has emerged as one of the major threats to security in recent years.

In order to anticipate the next significant cyberattack, experts in cyber security constantly monitor the activities taking place in this digital space. These cyberattacks can occur in any nation. Because millions of people worldwide are at risk, it is essential to be aware of them.

In addition to other popular locations like the deep web, TOR network, and i2p network, the dark web has become one of the busiest places for hackers to carry out illegal activities. This is interesting. Its ability to conceal a user's identity is the reason for its popularity. Utilising robust encryption technologies, this can be accomplished.

For many organisations, the use of encryption technologies to conceal sophisticated computer viruses that target hackers and cybercriminals is frequently regarded as a fundamental requirement. Any data that is sent over the internet is completely protected in this manner from malicious hackers. Additionally, this makes it difficult for cybercriminals to read confidential information and track any business customer activities. Customers can't be easily identified or their banking accounts can't be accessed by hackers.

It is the ideal location for hackers due to all of these characteristics. As a result, they have been launching worldwide attacks from the dark web base.

Ways Cyber Security Experts Use the Dark Web to Help Protect Businesses From Hacker Threats.

It's Critical to Understand How Hackers and Exploiters Work

The dark web is the best place to interact with hackers. The dark web isn't just for cyber criminals; cyber security professionals can also use it to increase business security.

The darknet is always used by hackers who want to take advantage of your company. This allows active cyber security professionals to easily track business information that hackers are selling. Utilising the dark web to avert major security problems is a proactive strategy. If you want to improve your security, it's best to use the dark web.

8 Ways Cyber security experts can improve business security using the dark web.

1. Gather Threat Information:
Dark web browsing never stops. There is always talk about major cyber security threats and potential threats from hacking groups. You can gain information that can be useful for your organisation by joining the right group.

With information gathered from the darknet, you can be prepared for potential security attacks as a security analyst. You can learn about the potential attack vector and attack mitigation strategies. By speaking with hackers and obtaining any pertinent information about their operations, you will also learn some new methods for dealing with security threats.

2. Hear from Hackers;
Members of the hacking group will discuss important information about their operations and the tools they use for hacking. In order to avoid attacks of a similar nature, you can gather this intelligence and thoroughly analyse it.

In order to ensure that your company's systems do not pose any threats, cyber security professionals must also comprehend how hackers operate. You will be able to take the necessary precautions to increase the security of your business if you have a thorough understanding of how the hackers operate.

3. Protect Information from Hackers; Legitimate businesses can defend themselves against hackers in a variety of ways. These hackers might

also try to hack into an organisation's systems to get sensitive information.

You can't stop these attacks. However, you can safeguard your valuable data from cybercriminals.

Through a comprehensive end-to-end security roadmap that includes monitoring, detecting, and managing threats, you can take certain measures to prevent the theft of sensitive information and its use for illegal purposes.

The dark web can help you protect your company's data with cyber security measures. Hackers will be less likely to pose a security threat as a result of this.

4. Protect the Privacy of Users; Whenever you use the internet, you expose yourself to hackers and make yourself an easy target. You are not only at risk from cybercrime, but you are also at risk from sharing private information with various government agencies and from monitoring user activities on the internet.

Understanding how these agencies can monitor user activities is crucial. This can be accomplished by gathering specific data about how they use the internet.

Your classified data will still be safe if you protect yourself from ISPs and other members of the local network. You can protect sensitive business data with strong privacy protection. Additionally, this will be useful for reducing security risks and enhancing business security.

5. Checking on employees who unintentionally share your business data online is another way to safeguard your organisation's data against the dark web.

Security experts can prevent a data breach by removing the company's information by actively surfing the darknet.

6. Protect Intellectual Property; Hackers attempt to obtain information about an organisation's intellectual

property. Any patent, signed
agreement, research details, and
clinical data may be included.

It is difficult for a hacking group to
obtain information of this high value.
However, the group has its own
methods by which it can obtain certain
details.

Cybercriminals can easily obtain these
business secrets in other ways.
Organisations' innovative concepts
must always be kept under lock and
key to prevent dark hackers from
stealing them.

7. Keep Your Organization's Data Safe Online;
You must always keep your organisation's data safe online. If not, it may open the door to a variety of cyberattacks on your company's systems.

You can forestall this sort of assault by eliminating or covering your information before it's distributed on the web. This will lower the likelihood that hackers will steal your data.

8. Protect Login Credentials;
You will also learn how to handle users' darknet login credentials. Users frequently do not secure their usernames and passwords, which makes them easy prey for cybercriminals. Phishing emails are another common method utilised by hackers to steal user login information.

Users must be educated about such attacks. Teach them how to reduce the likelihood that hackers will steal their login credentials.

How Organisations Move to the Dark Web to Improve Security Some organisations are constructing sites on the dark web to enhance security. However, doing so may make it more challenging for common users to access sites like Facebook and Amazon. These dark web sites are used to protect users from cybercriminals, marketing firms, and governments that track user information.

Additionally, it permits users to access platforms that block networks in China, Cuba, and North Korea.

In order to stay out of the way of potential competitors and hackers, some private businesses even have their very own dark web site. After migrating to the cloud, many businesses are moving to the dark web, but bad actors are targeting them. As a result, they came to the conclusion that their organisation's clients and customers required more privacy or security.

Marketing can benefit greatly from moving to the dark web. By reading a large number of completed online forms, marketers can use the dark web to learn about potential customer needs and wants.

Traditional marketing methods will be affected as more businesses use the dark web. This is because marketers won't be able to obtain precise customer data. Additionally, as more customers utilise TOR browsers and other hidden networks, analytics will become less accurate.

However, marketers must exercise caution when navigating the dark web. It contains a great deal of sensitive, criminal, and additive information that has the potential to harm an organisation's image as well as the brand image of its employees.

CONCLUSION

If you don't use Tor (The Onion Router) and a premium VPN (Virtual Private Network) like ExpressVPN, browsing the Dark Web can be risky. The Tor browser is a safe one that encrypts your data and routes your connection through the Onion network of volunteer-run servers to keep you anonymous online. However, this browser does not prevent your ISP from recognizing that you are using Tor itself.

Using the darknet is a practical way to improve your organisation's security posture. But only if you take preventive security measures, including darknet monitoring, conducting regular penetration testing to find any vulnerabilities in your network and implementing regular security awareness training for all employees to educate your workforce about how to spot and report cyber threats.

These hacks can cause major setbacks to your organisation. And it's important to take such preventive measures to minimise the number of cyber-attacks. You can also protect your organisation's data from hackers by using strong security measures.

The best thing about using the darknet is learning how your critical business information can be protected from hackers and cyber criminals.